Legendary Ladies

Legendary Ladies

50 Goddesses to Empower and Inspire You

Ann Shen

CHRONICLE BOOKS

SAN FRANCISCO

Library of Congress Cataloging-in-Publication Data available.

ISBN: 978-1-4521-6341-3

Manufactured in China

Design by Jennifer Tolo Pierce

10 9 8 7 6 5

Chronicle books and gifts are available at special quantity discounts to
corporations, professional associations, literacy programs, and other
organizations. For details and discount information, please contact our
corporate/premiums department at corporatesales@chroniclebooks.com
or at 1-800-759-0190.

Chronicle Books LLC
680 Second Street
San Francisco, California 94107
www.chroniclebooks.com

For Lucy
and my
grandmothers

Contents

LOVE

POWER

PROTECTION

REINVENTION

Introduction

Mythology is a funny thing. When you really think about it, mythology is, at the root—with all due respect to that which is sacred and religious—stories that we have told ourselves about our own origins. Humans have long searched for answers about how we came to be, why we came to be, and what our purpose is. We've experienced many of the same struggles, no matter the trappings of our time and place in history. Mythology reveals all this. It unveils our truest desires, our greatest needs, and our most painful experiences: it lays it bare at our feet and reveals the truth about ourselves and the cultures that have shaped and interpreted these myths. Maybe even better than history and facts have done—because myths tell us more about what's truly important to us and what a culture's ideals are.

Goddesses have been a part of mythology since the very beginning, many responsible for creating the world as we know it. The divine feminine is often the force of life itself, from which we all stem, and working with it is a way to acknowledge the creator in each of us and the spirit of protection, courage, and love. Many of the goddesses have tales of overcoming, of manifesting—creating things from the power of thought alone—and of unflappable strength. While their stories and dominions vary, the goddesses here have one great common thread: they have all found their own power. And through their stories, and perhaps a little bit of faith and magic, they will empower you.

In the pages that follow, there's a diverse range of goddesses from many major pantheons across the globe. They represent the things that we value and seek in our lives: creativity, manifestation, love, power, protection, and reinvention. Their stories are wildly diverse; yet some are similar across great distances, illustrating what we value despite borders between us.

Here you will find primordial goddesses who existed before time itself, playful divinities who love to intervene with our mortal coils, and your greatest champions. Many have stories of great adventure, of courage, of sacrifice. All have stories that will help guide you in your everyday life.

Throughout, a common thread runs: that the masculine does not exist without the feminine, that they are two parts of every living being on Earth. Recent history has been largely patriarchal, which means the divine feminine has been oppressed for much too long. Hopefully you will find a patron goddess (or many) in here with whom you can connect—for guidance, for growth, for strength, or for whatever you need at this stage in your life. Use the categories to find a goddess to help you through where you are currently; refer back often as your life changes. Or simply enjoy their stories and be emboldened by this long history of women who have been integral in the foundation of many civilizations.

The divine feminine has always been here and will continue to be a part of our stories. Now it's up to you to honor it within yourself, because you are a descendent of these wild, willful women. These are our collective mothers, after all.

Creativity and Manifestation

Aditi

ORIGIN: *Hindu*

MYTHOLOGY: Mother of the endless universe, Aditi is one of the earliest sky goddesses in the Hindu pantheon. Her name translates to "limitless," just like her reach and powers. She existed before time and is said to be the goddess of the past and the future, controlling all of time. Aditi is also the source of the stars, suns, planets, and moons and then gave birth to twelve Adityas, who were spirits that became the twelve Zodiac signs. They take turns ruling the cosmos by month and created all the gods and goddesses. She's known as the Mother Cow and Cow of Light, as she nurtures the universe and is sometimes depicted as a cow.

 Call on Aditi when you want to create your own world of happiness.

Athena

ORIGIN: *Greek (Roman: Minerva)*

MYTHOLOGY: Daughter of Zeus, Athena is the Greek goddess of wisdom, arts, and war, making her a triple threat and a central figure of feminine and intellectual strength. In Greek legend, Athena sprang fully grown, wearing her golden armor, from Zeus's head after he swallowed her pregnant mother, Metis. Athena competed with Poseidon to be the patron god of the Greek capital. Poseidon gave them the gift of a saltwater well, which they could not drink from. Athena gave them an olive tree—which provided shade from the sun, oil for their lamps, and olives to eat. It's no wonder the capital city then became Athens and she its deity. Today, the olive branch still serves as a universal symbol of peace.

Although known as the goddess of war, Athena represents the reason and strategy aspect of battle. She's often portrayed with an owl on her right shoulder, representing wisdom, and Medusa on her shield, representing Athena's ties to earlier mythologies from pre-Greek cultures. Athena is also credited with gifting the world with art, and teaching humans weaving, pottery, and architecture. The Parthenon is the most famous temple built in honor of Athena—her wisdom guided architects in building it—and it stood as a tribute to her famous virtue and sexual modesty, a divergence from the Greek gods' typical romantic involvements.

 Call on Athena when you need to access your inner intuition and wisdom.

Benten

ORIGIN: *Japanese*

MYTHOLOGY: Also known as Benzaiten, Benten is the Japanese sea goddess of eloquence and beauty. Talent, wealth, wisdom, romance, and music all fall under her domain. She was the only goddess among the Seven Gods of Good Fortune, a group of gods who traveled together on a treasure ship, and the only one who grants good luck and happiness. She's also the patron goddess of geishas and lovers of art.

Daughter of a dragon king, Benten married another dragon who was terrorizing the island of Enoshima by eating children. His love for her transformed him into a perfect gentleman. Together, they live in Lake Biwa, which is shaped like and named after her favorite instrument, a short-necked lute. Benten is often depicted riding a dragon and playing a biwa, with white snakes as her messengers—so it's good luck in Japanese culture to see a white snake.

 Call on Benten when you need an extra boost of luck on your side—especially when it comes to creative endeavors.

Chang-o

ORIGIN: *Chinese*

MYTHOLOGY: Chang-o is the Chinese goddess of the moon, where she resides with a rabbit and a three-legged toad. Before her current residency, Chang-o lived on Earth with her husband, Yi, an archer, and was an attendant of the goddess Hsi Wang Mu. When Yi shot nine of the ten suns out of the sky, the couple was stripped of their deity status as punishment. Chang-o begged Hsi Wang Mu to help them out of their mortal sentence with her magic peaches, and Hsi Wang Mu took pity on them by making two elixirs from her fruit to make them immortal, though not gods, again. Chang-o decided to drink both potions, hoping to become a goddess with the extra dose of magic but instead became so light she floated up to the moon. She did indeed become a goddess again, but she is now forever tied to the moon. Her husband built her a cinnamon-wood palace there and can only visit once a month on the night of the new moon.

The annual Moon Festival, also known as the Autumn Harvest Festival, is held in celebration of Chang-o and the power of the divine feminine force of yin in yin and yang. People hold rituals in which they light incense for Chang-o's altar while whispering their heart's secret wish; then they remain quiet until they hear the first word uttered by a passerby, which is Chang-o's answer.

 Call on Chang-o when you're seeking the answer to your secret wish or question, especially during a full moon.

the Muses

ORIGIN: *Greek*

MYTHOLOGY: Daughters of Zeus and Mnemosyne, the goddess of memory, the nine goddesses overseeing arts and sciences are also known as the Muses. According to legend, they were born on the mountain of Parnassus, and many poets and scholars would travel there to drink from a spring that ran down the mountain, to gain divine inspiration.

Each of the Muses oversees a different aspect of creativity: Calliope is poetry; Clio, history; Euterpe, lyrical poetry; Melpomene, tragedy; Thalia, comedy; Terpsichore, dance; Polyhymnia, music and storytelling; Urania, astronomy; and Erato, erotic poetry and mime. However, if one Muse is present, anyone can petition them for their inspiration in any aspect. Gifting mortal endeavors with their divine spirit, Muses are loving and joyful, often singing songs of praise. They also bestow mortals with talent and skill. Often they're worshipped with milk, honey, and wine. Modern museums originated as shrines to the Muses.

Call on the Muses when you're looking for inspiration and a boost in your talent; especially the one who oversees your specific area.

Saraswati

ORIGIN: *Hindu*

MYTHOLOGY: A personification of one of the most important rivers in India, Saraswati is the Hindu goddess of knowledge, music, and arts. Legendary for her beauty and grace, she's known for her brilliant white skin, which represents the light of knowledge. She is often portrayed with four arms holding the symbols of her domain: a book (representing education), a vina (an Indian lute, representing music), and a strand of beads or a ritual pot (representing spiritual knowledge). She's celebrated during a festival in the spring, Vasant Panchami, where people worship her to achieve enlightenment through knowledge and wear saffron-colored robes to echo the mustard blooms in the fields. During this festival, children are often taught to write for the first time, as she created the Sanskrit alphabet.

Her companion is a white swan (*hamsa*), who in myth is believed to be able to separate milk from water—a representation of Saraswati's ability to separate good from evil. She travels on the swan, an animal that's a symbol of spiritual perfection and transcendence, so she's also called Hamsavāhini, meaning "she who has a hamsa as her vehicle." Ceremonies and prayers are performed for Saraswati by students and artists alike before they begin a new endeavor.

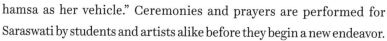 *Call on Saraswati when you need intellectual enlightenment and an extra blessing in creative pursuits.*

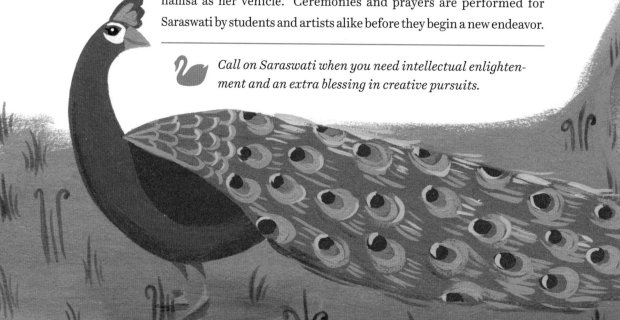

Spider Woman

ORIGIN: *Southwestern Native American*

MYTHOLOGY: Especially sacred to southwestern Native American tribes such as the Hopi and Navajo, Spider Woman is a creation goddess who spun a web that created the directions north, south, west, and east. As she wove her web, she created all living things on Earth, including the mountains, waters, and deserts, thus connecting the different regions. In this new world, she had two daughters, Ut Set and Nau Ut Set, who made the sun, moon, and stars to light the way. Spider Woman also created all the people on Earth by molding them out of different-colored clays. While she is called Spider Woman, her real name is uttered only during sacred ceremonies.

Also known as Spider Grandmother, Spider Woman is additionally a thought goddess, and anything she visualized came into creation. She holds the threads that connect the mortal world with the divine.

 Call on Spider Woman while meditating and accessing your crown chakra to tap into her thread that connects you to the universe. She will provide you with the universal energy you need to manifest your goals.

Tyche

ORIGIN: *Greek (Roman: Fortuna)*

MYTHOLOGY: Goddess of fortune and luck, Tyche is a blind goddess who is often portrayed with a blindfold over her eyes. This is a nod to fortune not discriminating upon whom it bestows luck; and it also refers to Tyche's following her intuition rather than her sight to better determine the wind of fate. The daughter of Titan gods Oceanus and Tethys, Tyche gained immortality and was elevated to a goddess by Zeus after she helped him save Olympus from Gaia's schemes during a battle with the Titans. She's often portrayed with a wheel of destiny and a cornucopia, as she oversees both the direction of one's luck and the abundance of life. A fickle goddess, Tyche can turn one's fortunes quickly.

In her shrines, worshippers can get their fortunes told, as she also oversees oracles. Since soldiers adored her and often carried her symbols into battle, her legend spread across many continents.

Call on Tyche when you want good luck and fortune on your side. Make her traditional offerings with honey, milk, and cakes in the shape of a wheel.

Love

Aphrodite

ORIGIN: *Greek (Roman: Venus)*

MYTHOLOGY: The illustrious goddess of love and beauty, Aphrodite arose fully grown out of sea foam in a scallop shell, on which she sailed to the island of Cyprus. Her name translates into "she who rises from the waves." She was known for her magical embroidered girdle that could seduce any lover, and she had them in spades—including Ares, god of war, and Adonis, who became the god of beauty and desire. Jealous of her love for the beautiful mortal Adonis, Ares turned into a wild boar and killed the man while he was hunting. When she discovered the body of her beloved, Aphrodite cried over him, sprinkling his blood with nectar and causing anemones to spring out of the ground around him. This is the reason why the flowers have such brief and fragile blooms. Moved by her devoted love, Zeus allowed Adonis to become a god who lives in the Underworld for half the year, and on Earth with Aphrodite for the other half.

Aphrodite also loves company and often travels with fun-loving spirits, including her attendants the Three Graces: Joyous, Brilliance, and Flowering. The Graces exemplify the gifts she bestows upon mere mortals if she chooses to smile upon them: joy, brilliance, and abundance. To help mortals find romantic love, she gifts them with a bit of her charm and appeal. Her sacred plants are myrtles, roses, and anemones. Many Greeks wore wreaths of myrtle on their wedding day for Aphrodite's blessing.

Call on Aphrodite when you need more love in your life—be it for self-care or falling in love. Attract her attention by burning her favorite scents, frankincense and myrrh.

Creiddylad

ORIGIN: *Welsh*

MYTHOLOGY: Goddess of flowers and spring, Creiddylad is an eternal May Queen who's celebrated during the Spring solstice. Her legend starts with her hand promised to Gwythr ap Greidawl, a handsome and brave Welsh warrior she loved, but before they could be married, she was abducted by Gwyn ap Nudd, Lord of the Underworld. Gwythr built up an army to rescue her, but King Arthur intervened and decreed that the two men would have to fight over her twice every year, the battles taking place at the turn of seasons. So at the start of each spring, Creiddylad is celebrated as she returns to the surface of the earth and is reunited with her love, and her joy covers the world in blooms. When she returns to the Underworld, the earth turns to winter.

Creiddylad's story represents self being the only constant as time moves and seasons change, and she reminds us all that self-love comes before anything else. She always carries abundance within her, blessing everything around her with new life.

Call on Creiddylad when you need a loving spirit to guide you into a better relationship with yourself; especially while you are practicing self-care.

Freya

ORIGIN: *Scandinavian*

MYTHOLOGY: The Norse goddess of love and ruler of war and death, Freya is a beautiful sorceress who rides around in a cat-drawn golden chariot. According to her legend, she was born to mediate the conflict between two warring groups of Norse gods: the peaceful Vanir and the combative Aesir. She joined the Vanir hostages in Asgard, home of the Aesir gods, quickly won them over with her charm, and established a spiritual peace. She wears a falcon-feathered cloak that allows her to travel swiftly between heaven and Earth. On the battlefield, she had first choice of the souls who would come and live with her in her enormous palace in Asgard, where they celebrated forever in joy and pleasure.

Because of her beauty and love of pleasure, she was also famous for her sexuality in many of her myths. In one myth, she is obsessed with obtaining the famous amber necklace, Brísingamen, from the four dwarves who forged it. She loved the beautiful necklace the moment she set eyes on it, and the four dwarves asked that she pay for it by sleeping with each of them—beauty for beauty.

Call on Freya when you need the push to be bold and embark on an adventure to pursue your heart's desire.

Hathor

ORIGIN: *Egyptian*

MYTHOLOGY: The ancient Egyptian goddess of love and joy, Hathor has been worshipped for more than 3,000 years. Nicknamed the Gentle Cow of Heaven, she provided milk for her son, Ra the Sun God, and all the pharaohs of Egypt, which made them divine. She also created the Milky Way from the milk in her breasts. She's often portrayed wearing a crown with a solar disk rimmed by two cow horns. Worshipped by royalty and common folk alike, Hathor is celebrated at joyful ceremonies of music and dance. Hathor was the most beloved goddess of all in the Egyptian pantheon and had the most festivals in her honor.

Because of her loving nature, Hathor is also the goddess of the Underworld, where she waits under the branches of sycamore trees to usher souls into the afterlife. The Golden One, as she is also known, is the protector of all females and champion of romantic bonds. She's a shape-shifter who can appear in the form of Seven Hathors; these spirits appear at the births of babies and can foretell their futures. Her symbols are the sistrum, a rattle in the shape of an ankh, and the hand mirror.

 Call on Hathor when you're looking to spark more joy in your romantic life, especially when starting new love affairs.

Isis

ORIGIN: *Egyptian*

MYTHOLOGY: Goddess of magic, Isis is one of the most venerated goddesses in Egyptian history. Through her amazing powers, she's able to shape-shift into many different types of animals—and was a character in many myths throughout different cultures, earning her the title "Lady of Ten Thousand Names." Isis performs all types of miracles; she can resurrect the dead, give fertility, and cure the sick. A blessed healer, Isis taught humans the great medicinal qualities of plants to cure diseases.

The most famous story about Isis involves her beloved Osiris, who was both her husband and brother. Jealous of their great love, their brother Set murdered Osiris, placed his body in a coffin, and buried it under a tree. Isis searched high and low to find Osiris, and when she finally did, Set stole the body again and cut it into fourteen pieces, scattering them all over Egypt. In great grief, Isis transformed into a falcon and found all the pieces of her husband—except for his penis. Using her magical powers, she bonded all the pieces together with wax and formed a new penis for him out of gold, bringing him back to life. Reunited briefly, they conceived a child together—the falcon-headed god Ra, who in turn brought vengeance upon Set.

 Call on Isis when you need strength to heal a broken heart and for the power to find hope again.

Laka

ORIGIN: *Hawai'ian*

MYTHOLOGY: With her name meaning "gentle, docile, attraction," Laka is a beautiful Polynesian goddess of love and wilderness. Inventor of the hula dance, Laka taught humans the art of the hula as a means of telling stories, preserving the history of the Hawai'ian people, and honoring different gods and goddesses. She is married to the fertility god Lono, who came down to Earth on a rainbow to marry her. The rain connects the two of them, so rain is a sacred time for Laka.

Dancers in training still build altars to Laka in the hula halaus, where they practice before a performance. Filled with Laka's favorite flowers and plants, like maile, hala pepe, 'ie 'ie, ki, 'ôhia lehua, and palai, the offerings are taken down to the ocean and released after the performances, thanking Laka for her blessing.

 Call on Laka when you want to attract love or wealth into your life; she will help ground you and reveal a path to abundance.

Oshun

ORIGIN: *Yoruba*

MYTHOLOGY: Oshun is a goddess of sweet waters, and her dominion is love, beauty, and creation. She is one of the seven major orishas (divine spirits in the Yoruba religion, of which there are fourteen total), and the namesake of a river in West Africa. Legend has it that she's the source of power for all the other orishas. Oshun makes all things flow in the universe, through both her love and her strength. She was sent by the other orishas to intervene with Ogun, the orisha of tools and father of civilization, who had grown tired of creating and caused the world to stop growing. Oshun was the only one who could lift his spirits and encourage him to begin creating again. Oshun is also the only goddess who can carry messages between the mortal world and the Supreme Creator in heaven.

In Nigeria, there is an annual ceremony called Ibo-Osun where women of the village dance for the goddess during a feast of yams. The best dancer wins Oshun's favor and is chosen to become the village adviser on healing and fertility—two of the goddess's domains. Oshun's love for beautiful, luxurious things serves as a reminder to appreciate the pleasures and love in our own lives.

 Call on Oshun when you need to forgive and heal in love, and to bring renewal into your life. Wear yellow and brass or copper jewelry to channel her spirit.

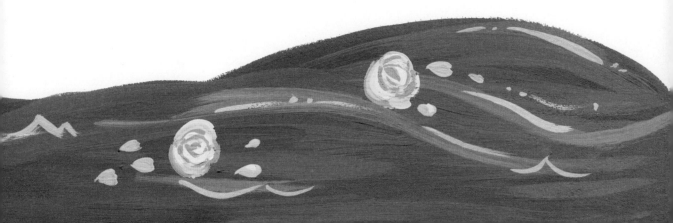

Parvati

ORIGIN: *Hindu*

MYTHOLOGY: The golden Hindu goddess of love and devotion, Parvati forms a holy trinity with Saraswati, goddess of knowledge, and Lakshmi, goddess of fortune. According to the legend, Parvati was born in the Himalayan mountains, as daughter of King Himavat and Queen Minavati. She is the embodiment of nurturing feminine energy, in complement to her husband, Shiva, the god of chaos and regeneration. Worshipped for her patience and determination, Parvati won Shiva over by ascending into the mountains and practicing asceticism until he couldn't resist her and spent all his time trying to please her. She was also regarded for her strength and ferocity; when the hero Kartikeya, who was a son of Shiva, became a lust-filled monster raping all the women he encountered, Parvati cursed him, so that every time he attempted to rape a woman, she turned into Parvati's likeness—and that ended his rampage.

In another legend, Parvati grew tired of Shiva making fun of her for her dark skin, so she went into the mountains and once again practiced asceticism until Brahma came to grant her wish. She wanted to be golden-skinned, so he blessed her by separating her darkness—which then manifested, fully sprung, as the goddess Kali. Now Parvati has more than one hundred different incarnations, depending on her mood. Parvati is also known for the creation of her son Ganesha, the benevolent elephant-headed god of wisdom who removes obstacles.

 Call on Parvati for spiritual strength and persistence to pursue your romantic goals.

Psyche

ORIGIN: *Greek*

MYTHOLOGY: Goddess of soul, Psyche started life as a mortal woman. Her beauty was so unparalleled that men began to worship her instead of Aphrodite, which angered the jealous goddess of love. In an attempt to humiliate Psyche, Aphrodite ordered her son, Eros, to use his love arrows to make the mortal fall in love with a hideous man. However, when the god of love saw her, he fell in love and stole her away to be his secret bride. He built a beautiful palace for her, where she was alone except in the evening when he would come to their bed, shrouded by darkness and mystery. She never saw his face nor knew who he was. They were happy together for a while, but on a visit home, Psyche's sisters planted a seed of doubt in her mind. So one night, to learn his identity, she secretly lit a candle when Eros was asleep. She was so entranced by his beautiful face that she didn't notice when candle wax dripped on him, waking him up. He was so angry about her betrayal that he fled, and the palace fell to ashes.

Devastated over her loss, Psyche sought out the only person who would know Eros's whereabouts—his vain mother. Aphrodite looked unkindly upon Psyche and gave her near-impossible tasks before she would reveal Eros's location: sorting a roomful of seeds over one night, catching the sun sheep's fleece, collecting water from the River Styx, and traveling to Hades to borrow Persephone's beauty salve. Completing each task tirelessly, Psyche finally faltered on her return from Hades. Unable to resist the lure of Persephone's magical salve, she opened the box—and the salve killed her, its powers too strong for a mortal. Eros swooped down and carried her to Olympus, where he begged Zeus for her life. Zeus gave her a cup of ambrosia that not only revived her but made her a goddess; the two lovers lived together ever after, having two children, named Pleasure and Delight. Because of her transcendence from mortal to goddess, Psyche is often portrayed with butterfly wings.

 Call on Psyche for the strength to persevere through dark challenges in pursuit of what you love. Working with her will be a practice in uniting your heart and soul to find your own inner divinity.

Power

Áine

ORIGIN: *Celtic*

MYTHOLOGY: The sun goddess of love and light, Áine is a fairy queen from Ireland, and the county of Limerick is especially sacred to her. She rules over agriculture and animals, and she's celebrated every year at the Midsummer Festival. People light torches and run up her hill, Cnoc Áine, to ask for her blessing on their farms. It's believed that she and her fairy folk are celebrating the festival on the other side of the hill, and sometimes she will appear to young girls and lead them to the fairy festivities.

As a strong and loving goddess, Áine is also a survivor of sexual abuse in many myths and she guides her people—especially women—to the warmth of the sun, to finding their own power, and to regeneration. In one story, Áine was raped by King Ailill Aulom of Munster; she bit off his ear, which made him ineligible for the throne. In another, Gerald, Earl of Desmond, stumbled upon her bathing in a lake and stole her cloak so that she would marry him. When she refused, Gerald raped her and in her fury, she turned him into a goose. However, from that union she gave birth to a gifted son who became known as Merlin.

Áine is portrayed with flowing red hair and a headband of stars, often wearing yellow and with her animals around her: a red mare, a rabbit, and a swan. According to another legend, she can transform into a red mare able to outrun anyone.

 Call on Áine to help you find your own inner strength to face present challenges or overcome past traumas.

Amaterasu

ORIGIN: *Shinto*

MYTHOLOGY: Sun goddess Amaterasu was born from the left eye of the god Izanagi. She had dominion over the land and sea; she was the warmth and beauty of the sun. A benevolent protector and provider for humans, she gifted them with rice, silk, and fabric. However, she constantly feuded with her brother Susano-o, god of storms—a rivalry that came to a head when their father banished Susano-o from heaven. In response, her brother went on a rampage and destroyed Amaterasu's rice fields, piled feces on her throne, and threw the flayed skin of a horse (her sacred animal) into her weaving workshop, killing one of her handmaidens.

Disgusted and furious, Amaterasu went into hiding in a cave, shutting the light of the sun in with her. In darkness, all life on Earth then began to die, and the kami (Shinto divine beings) started to worry. Millions of kami gathered outside her cave, pleading for her to come out, but to no avail. Finally, Uzume, spirit of joy, began dancing and attracted the attention of all the kami, who laughed, sang, and cheered with the beautiful dancer. When Amaterasu called out to ask what was happening, someone told her another goddess had come to replace her. Curiosity got the best of her; she peeked out of the cave and stared right into a magic mirror that the kami had constructed outside. Never having seen her reflection before, she was momentarily entranced by her own beauty. The other kami seized the opportunity to pull her out of the cave and restore her to her throne. Because of Amaterasu's importance, Japan is called the Land of the Rising Sun, and all emperors are said to be her descendents.

 Call on Amaterasu when you want to recognize the power within yourself and find the courage to let it shine.

Artemis

ORIGIN: *Greek (Roman: Diana)*

MYTHOLOGY: The Greek goddess of the hunt, wilderness, and moon, Artemis is the fierce protector of all wild creatures and the forest. At the age of three, she asked her father Zeus for a bow and arrow, a saffron hunting tunic, and hunting dogs, and she set off to live in the forest. She also asked never to be forced to marry. Because of her independence and strength, Artemis is often a patron goddess to young girls from the age of nine until marriage. Followers celebrated her at an annual ancient festival that took place in Brauron, near the Aegean sea, where her sacred temple stood. Young men and women performed a ritual wild bear dance to express their free spirit. Artemis traveled with a band of Nymphs, and she frequently held festival nights that involved erotic dancing and masquerades.

A skilled huntress, Artemis was equally loved and feared by all. In one legend, Orion was her hunting partner; but when he attempted to rape her, she killed him, and he became a constellation in the night sky, which she rules. While she herself had forsaken marriage and procreation, Artemis was associated with fertility after midwifing the birth of her twin brother, Apollo, who is the complement of masculinity and the sun to her femininity and the moon. She is often called upon to help guide women through difficult childbirth. She wears a crescent-moon tiara as a symbol of her sovereignty over the wilderness; and her animals are deer, bears, and boars.

Call on Artemis when you need help focusing like a hunter on your goals and for spiritual strength.

Demeter

ORIGIN: *Greek (Roman: Ceres)*

MYTHOLOGY: Goddess of the harvest, Demeter is best known for the story that involves her daughter, Persephone, queen of the Underworld. In love with Persephone's beauty, Hades, god of the Underworld, abducted her one day. Demeter searched high and low for her daughter; and in her grief, the plants and crops began to wither and die. Eventually Hecate, the goddess of magic, was able to help Demeter locate Persephone in the Underworld. When Hecate went to negotiate Persephone's freedom, Hades said she could leave if she had eaten nothing in the Underworld. Unfortunately, Persephone had eaten some pomegranate seeds; so she was required to return to Hades every year. At those times, Demeter grieves, and the world withers into fall and winter; when Persephone reunites with her mother, spring and summer bloom.

During her search for Persephone, Demeter went to the town of Eleusis in Greece. There, she acted as a nursemaid for the king's two sons. In gratitude, she planned to make one immortal by putting him in a fire to slowly burn away his mortal self. However, the queen caught her and screamed in horror, causing Demeter to abandon the ritual. She revealed to them then that she was a divine goddess; and she decided to thank them instead by teaching them to plant, harvest, and grow grains—bringing the gift of agriculture to humanity.

 Call on Demeter for her blessings when you want to plant, harvest, and grow your deepest dreams into reality; also ask for her strength in pursuit of what you desire.

Eos

ORIGIN: *Greek (Roman: Aurora)*

MYTHOLOGY: Titan goddess of dawn, Eos pulls back the curtain of night, ushering away her sister, Selene, goddess of the moon, and bringing out her brother, Helios, god of the sun, to start the day. Depicted with rosy fingers, saffron-colored robes, a brilliant tiara, and feathered wings, Eos was a beautiful goddess who had many love affairs. Most were with handsome young men she would abduct from the mortal world.

Through her long-standing romance with Astraeus (Titan god of dusk), she had four children, the four winds: Boreas, the north wind; Notus, the south wind; Zephyrus, the west wind; and Eurus, the east wind. She often rides a golden chariot, or flies with her own wings, carrying a torch to light the skies pink and bring on the dawn, chasing away all evil nocturnal spirits.

 Call on Eos when you want assistance lighting the way for your life's path, and for her light to chase away your own inner demons.

Gaia

ORIGIN: *Greek (Roman: Terra)*

MYTHOLOGY: Born of the universal chaos that existed before everything else, Gaia is the mother goddess who created all life, according to Greek mythology. The embodiment of Mother Earth herself, she created the mountains, the sea, and the sky. The sky was named Uranus, and she took him as a lover. Together, Gaia and Uranus had powerful children, the Titans, including Chronos (time). Gaia was so in love with the world she was creating with her children that Uranus became wildly jealous. Growing tired of him, she created a sickle and gave it to her son Chronos to take care of the problem. Chronos used it to cut off Uranus's genitals. When Uranus's blood fell into the sea, more children in the Greek pantheon sprang up, including the Furies, the Giants, and the Nymphs. Gaia existed before Zeus and all the other gods; they are the children of her children.

Gaia represents wild and raw nature, and she's associated with expressing her rage through earthquakes to remind us that the earth is a living presence. The Greeks built many temples near deep chasms in the ground to connect more closely with her; her most sacred temple was in Delphi. Followers worshipped her by offering barley and honey cakes in her sacred caves or in holes inside the ground. They perform these rituals before harvesting or extracting from the earth.

 Call on Gaia when you need nurturing support through a tough time in your life; empower yourself through nature by going outside or planting your bare feet on the earth.

Lakshmi

ORIGIN: *Hindu*

MYTHOLOGY: The Hindu goddess of fortune and prosperity, Lakshmi is said to have been born floating on a lotus at the creation of the universe. In Hinduism, a male god is passive until paired with a female goddess whose energy activates his power. Lakshmi is paired with Vishnu, who gives life and protection to all on Earth—and they have always been together, through many incarnations in myth.

Patron to the wealth of Earth and soul, this golden goddess is often portrayed with four arms to represent the four Hindu goals of life: kāma (love), dharma (morals and ethics), artha (purpose), and moksha (self-knowledge and liberation). Cows are one of her sacred animals since they represent the hard work and labor that she favors in one's pursuit of earthly abundance. Owls and elephants are also her animals, because owls represent the perseverance to see through the darkness and the unknown, and elephants represent work ethic and strength.

Lakshmi is celebrated and worshipped during Diwali, the Hindu festival of lights. People clean and decorate their homes with bright lights and dress themselves in beautiful new clothes to attract her favor. She's often portrayed wearing red robes embroidered with brilliant gold, and draped in the most beautiful jewels and pearls.

Call on Lakshmi when you need to persevere toward your goals and keep moving forward.

Liễu Hạnh

ORIGIN: *Vietnamese*

MYTHOLOGY: A fairy princess daughter of the Jade Emperor, the Taoist Supreme Deity, Liễu Hạnh was sent to Earth to live out life as a mortal girl after breaking a precious jade bowl in her heavenly home. In her earthly home in Tien Huong Village in Vietnam, Liễu Hạnh grew to love humans and met a kind man whom she married. She was reincarnated several times on Earth before her final ascent to heaven, when she chose to return to Earth as goddess of the celestial realm. Liễu Hạnh became a symbol of feminine divinity and strength, choosing to make her own way.

One of the Four Immortals, chief figures who are worshipped by the Vietnamese people in the Red River Delta region, Liễu Hạnh is also a goddess who oversees poetry, music, and painting—bringing these things to the mortal world. People worship her and ask for her blessings in talent and inspiration. She's associated with traditional chao van music, and when people play it, they connect with her. Liễu Hạnh blesses people who are good and punishes those who are malicious. Different rulers throughout Vietnam's history, hearing of her power, have sought to suppress Liễu Hạnh by burning down her temples; this made all the animals die of mysterious diseases, spreading panic among the villagers until they made her offerings and the government built her new temples. She is now the leading figure in the goddess cult Đạo Mẫu.

 Call on Liễu Hạnh to connect with divine feminine energy and for the power to make your own path.

Oya

ORIGIN: *Yoruba*

MYTHOLOGY: Goddess of the storms and winds, Oya is a powerful sorceress who controls the Niger River in Nigeria. She's married to the thunder god, Shango, and she sends winds to warn people about the arrival of her husband. Oya is also a shape-shifting goddess; she has appeared as an antelope or a water buffalo to join the mortal realm, then sheds the skin to appear as a mortal woman as she shops the marketplaces. A strong overseer of justice, Oya knocks any misuse of power to its knees.

Oya is a bringer of sudden change. She is also a goddess of rebirth—bringing those who worship her from darkness to light. As a guardian of women, she ushers the dead across the veil and guards the cemeteries. She can also call forth death or delay its arrival when people are at the end of their lives. Her association with the darkness and her tempestuous nature make her a powerful goddess of magic. Maroon and copper are her favorite colors; she's often depicted wearing a copper headdress and bracelets, while her followers wear maroon beads to invoke her blessings.

 Call on Oya when you need the strength to speak your truth; just as she controls the winds of nature, she also controls the wind of our breath.

Pele

ORIGIN: *Hawai'ian*

MYTHOLOGY: Pele is the Hawai'ian goddess of fire and creator of the Hawai'ian islands. One of many children of Haumea and Kanehoalani, the ambitious and tempestuous Pele was at constant odds with several of her siblings—especially the sea goddess Namaka. Pele often created hot spots of fire all over the islands, and Namaka was constantly extinguishing her flames. Their parents banished Pele, who then set off on a canoe with any other siblings who wanted to go with her—including cloud goddess Hi'iaka—and they made the islands of Hawai'i through her special talent for creating volcanoes. After being chased by Namaka, attempting to extinguish her trail of flames, Pele disappeared into the Kīlauea volcano where she now resides.

Pele's volcano is located on the island of Hawai'i, and is one of the most active volcanos in the world. Offerings of flowers, sugar cane, strawberries, and other gifts are thrown into her crater to stave off eruptions. She's an active, adaptable goddess who loves to interact with mortals throughout her islands. There are many urban legends surrounding her myth. Some claim that she appears as an old woman at night on island highways asking for a cigarette or as a red-robed woman dancing on the rim of the volcano. Pele blesses mortals with protection by providing warnings through her many manifestations. It's also easy to anger her. It's strongly believed that if you steal lava rocks from her volcanoes, Pele will curse you.

Call on Pele when you're looking for strength in following your own convictions.

Protection

Ala

ORIGIN: *Ibo*

MYTHOLOGY: Daughter of the Supreme Creator Chi, Ala is one of the most important Alusi (deities) in western Africa. She's the queen of life and death, and she brings abundance both in humans and in the earth as quickly as she takes it away. Ala is a keeper of morality for humans, and those who transgress and commit crimes will be punished by her. She often warns people first in dreams to change their ways, before she sends her army of ants.

The custom of burying our deceased in the ground comes from Ala's legend. She decreed that all souls be returned to her womb. She is often portrayed seated on a golden throne next to her husband, Amadioha, the sky Alusi. Her earthly messenger is the python, highly revered in Ibo communities.

 *Call on Ala when you want to find justice
or protection from those who harm you.*

Brigit

ORIGIN: *Irish*

MYTHOLOGY: A widely loved and respected goddess in Celtic times, Brigit is the sun goddess of creative arts, a matron of poetry, music, and smithcraft. As one of the prominent goddesses in Irish folklore, she also oversees wisdom, fertility, and healing.

Daughter of the fertility god the Dagda, she married Bres, an Irish king from a warring tribe, hoping to end the feud between their people. Sadly they did not succeed, and their three sons were sent into major battle between the two families. When her sons died, Brigit was the first person to "keen," and her wails of grief were heard so loudly throughout all of Ireland that it finally brought both sides to drop their weapons and forge a peace. Brigit is also credited with the invention of whistling, which both alerts her friends to come to her side and provides women with protection.

It's said that everywhere she walks, small flowers and shamrocks grow. She has an ancient temple in Kildare, where an eternal flame and miraculous healing well reside; the practice of throwing pennies into wells for wishes originated with her worship. Brigit is associated with the coming of spring, as her gifts bring light, inspiration, and the healing energy of the sun into the world. Every February 1, even now, she's celebrated during the festival of Imbolc in Ireland.

Call on Brigit to help bring peace into your heart, heal past pain, and light inspiration for a new path in life.

Durga

ORIGIN: *Hindu*

MYTHOLOGY: Known as the Invincible One, goddess of war Durga (also referred to as Devi or Shakti) was born out of the flaming breath of dozens of gods during the primordial war between gods and demons. Manifested as a bejeweled golden goddess with ten arms, each holding a weapon handed to her by the gods, Durga rode in on a tiger and swiftly slaughtered the buffalo demon leader, Mahishasura, and his demon army. Durga traditionally holds the weapons of all the male gods, since in Hindu belief, female goddess energy is what powers and charges everything.

A fierce protector, Durga is often depicted with a serene face while in battle because her strength comes from an act of love, of guarding those around her, and for liberating the souls who depend on her. She's celebrated during a ten-day festival in the autumn, the Durga Puja, and offered flowers, fruit, mangos, and marigold garlands.

 Call on Durga for protection when you are suffering spiritually, emotionally, or physically.

Hecate

ORIGIN: *Greek (Roman: Trivia)*

MYTHOLOGY: Goddess of magic and Queen of the Crossroads, Hecate is a moon divinity associated with the new moon. She is often accompanied by canines and portrayed with three heads. She is the keeper of the skeleton key that can open any portal and is thus also the gatekeeper of the Underworld. Ghosts are under her dominion, and she commands them as she pleases as the intermediary between the living and the dead. Hecate can be found where three crossroads diverge, and among cemeteries and crime scenes. Her legend states that since she is the witness to every crime, she is considered a great protectress and is worshipped and invoked for such.

Her power is honored above all others by Zeus, and she's a messenger between other deities. Once she stole a beauty salve from Hera to give to Hera's rival Europa. In a rage, Hera pursued Hecate but never caught her as she fled into the bed of a woman giving birth, then to a funeral, before diving into a lake in Hades, where she was cleansed and emerged stronger than ever. Thereafter, Hecate was a goddess of birth, death, and regeneration.

 Call on Hecate at night by candlelight when you are looking for protection; physical and spiritual. Canines are her spirit animal, and she often answers through them.

Kali

ORIGIN: *Indian*

MYTHOLOGY: Wild goddess of destruction, Kali existed before Hinduism came to India. She was rumored to have been born at the beginning of time, manifesting when demons threatened the earth. Kali is also known as a dark incarnation of the goddess Parvati. Her uncontrollable dance of destruction saved the world, but then began to destroy it until her beloved Shiva lay at her feet to help her regain control over her actions.

For those who worship Kali, she is a warm and loving mother figure. Depicted with black skin and a pointed tongue, Kali is a loyal guardian for those who call for her protection. She is responsible for life and death, and her powers bring protection, health, abundance, and fertility to her devotees. Kali's chaotic nature and her wild, disheveled snake hair speak to her primordial nature; and her extreme personality makes her difficult to understand. Her followers believe that to understand her is to be truly free from fear.

 Call on Kali when you're seeking protection and wanting to overcome fears.

Kuan Yin

ORIGIN: *Chinese*

MYTHOLOGY: Goddess of mercy and kindness, Kuan Yin began her life as a mortal princess named Maio Shan. Her cruel father, a king, had married her two older sisters off to wealthy but wicked men. Seeing their unhappiness, Kuan Yin asked to be sent to a temple to work and worship. The king complied, but ordered the temple residents to give her the most difficult menial tasks and make her work while others slept. All the animals around the temple saw the hardship she bore without complaint and came to help her. Tigers gathered firewood for the fire, snakes brought water, birds collected vegetables, and the spirit of fire cooked food. When Kuan Yin's father heard of the miracles occurring in the temple, he became angry and ordered her to be killed.

When Kuan Yin was ushered to the gates of the afterlife, she heard a cry of suffering from below. She decided to retain human form and became a bodhisattva (a person who can reach nirvana but chooses to delay it in order to help suffering souls). Her goodness transformed her into a goddess. Now just saying her name brings protection from harm. Often portrayed in a white gown and seated upon a lotus throne, Kuan Yin is a beloved divinity who bestows mercy and compassion on anyone who calls her name. She is a devout vegetarian, and her devotees will also follow her diet, especially on her sacred days.

Call on Kuan Yin when you are in need of compassion and mercy, whether from yourself or others.

Ma'at

ORIGIN: *Egyptian*

MYTHOLOGY: Ancient goddess of truth and justice, Ma'at oversees all that is right and moral. She has an important role in the afterlife judgment, where one's mortal heart is weighed against her ostrich feather on a scale. If the heart is equal to or lighter than her feather, the soul is then granted entrance to eternal life in Aaru, Egyptian paradise. If it weighs more than the feather, it is eaten by the demon Amit, and the soul is doomed to stay in Duat, the Egyptian Underworld.

Ma'at is tied closely with the sun-god Ra, as she is always watching over the mortal realm while he rises and sets over it. Egyptians live by the code of Ma'at, following her forty-two righteous moral declarations to ensure harmony and order in the universe. She is often portrayed as a beautiful woman with the wings of a falcon, wearing her famous ostrich feather as part of her headdress.

 Call on Ma'at when you are looking for a situation to be handled in a fair and just manner.

Mazu

ORIGIN: *Chinese*

MYTHOLOGY: Goddess of the sea, Mazu was born a mortal girl with extraordinary powers on the small island of Meizhou in Fujian Province, part of the strait between Taiwan and China. Miraculously, she didn't cry at birth, which led her parents to name her Lin Moniang, meaning "silent girl." She gained second sight—the ability to see visions of the future—when she visited a statue of the goddess Kuan Yin. At the age of thirteen, her extraordinary gift of predicting the weather led her to study under a Taoist monk who taught her charms and secret lore.

One of Mazu's most famous legends arose when she was sixteen: while she was weaving at home, she fell into a vision of her father and brother in trouble at sea. She projected herself to where they were and calmed the waves while guiding them to safety. However, her mother found Mazu's inanimate body on the floor at home and shook her, fearing that she was dead—which snapped Mazu out of her trance before she was able to rescue her father, who died. In her twenties, she transcended to heaven from a mountaintop, escorted over the rainbow by fairies, and became a protection goddess for all. People in trouble at sea reported seeing her appear dressed in red, controlling the weather and rescuing travelers from harm if they called her name.

 Call on Mazu when you are in trouble, especially while traveling or at sea, and she will guide you through rough times.

Rhiannon

ORIGIN: *Welsh*

MYTHOLOGY: A powerful goddess and fairy princess, Rhiannon appears to her followers on a magnificent white horse, dressed in royal robes. She is accompanied by her three birds from the Otherworld, and their songs have the power to lull someone to their sleeping death, restore the dead to life, or heal pain and sadness. And while her story is sad, she ultimately overcomes the obstacles in her path.

Although already betrothed to another by her fairy king and queen parents, Rhiannon decides she will marry the mortal king Pwyll, lord and hero of Dyfed. She leaves the fairy kingdom and appears to him on her glowing white horse, and he immediately is entranced. He chases her for three days but is unable to catch up to her, even though she never appears to increase her pace. Finally he implores her to stop, and she does. She introduces herself and then states her intent to marry him. They are swiftly married, and she moves into his mortal kingdom, a few years later having their first son.

Unfortunately, the newborn baby is abducted while the servants assigned to watch him were asleep. Fearing blame, the servants kill a puppy and smear the blood on the sleeping Rhiannon's face. As there are already rumors that she is a sorceress, this evidence leads Pwyll to believe that she has killed and eaten their baby. He punishes her by sending her to the stables, where she is forced to confess her crime to every traveler who passes through and to offer to carry them on her back like a horse. Meanwhile, a nearby lord kills a monster that had been frequently stealing his horse's foals from the barn. The monster leaves behind a baby boy on the doorstep. This child grows at a superhuman rate, and the lord and his wife recognize the child's resemblance to the mortal king and return him to his rightful parents. Rhiannon is cleared of the accusations and restored as queen.

 Call on Rhiannon for the strength to overcome your enemies and to find the magic within to pursue your desires.

Tara

ORIGIN: *Hindu*

MYTHOLOGY: Goddess of compassion and protection, Tara is one of the most beloved and preeminent divinities, and she is known to many Eastern religions. She was born of a single tear from the eye of Bodhisattva Avalokitesvara after he looked down from heaven at the suffering of humanity below. The moment the tear fell onto his palm, Tara sprang up fully formed, bringing courage and hope. Some legends also state that she was reincarnated as a mortal princess, who meditated to the ultimate level of enlightenment—and insisted on remaining in female form for all her reincarnations despite warnings from monks that she had to become a male in order to reach her true potential. Tara embodies the feminine divine and is manifested in as many as twenty-one different forms, most often associated with a color.

Green Tara is one of the most popular and active manifestations of the goddess. Considered the strongest and original goddess, Green Tara is a protector from all negative energy and from eight noted dangers: lions and pride; elephants and delusion; fire and hatred; snakes and envy; thieves and fanaticism; prisons and greed; water disasters and lust; and demons and doubt. A bringer of joy, Tara is also a healer and a granter of wishes. She is often depicted sitting on a lotus at peace, with her right leg extended to symbolize her ability to spring into action.

 Call on Tara for immediate assistance. She is a goddess of speed, and she empowers your inner wisdom to help save yourself.

Yemoja

ORIGIN: *Yoruba*

MYTHOLOGY: Also known as Mama Watta ("mother of the water") in the African diaspora where her legend has spread, Yemoja is a Yoruba orisha, a divine spirit, who gave birth to life on Earth. Thus she is goddess of the living waters, meaning the oceans, and mother of fourteen orishas.

While mostly known for being even-tempered, when angered Yemoja can be violent and relentless like a storm in the ocean. Since she oversees all life in the water, she is often represented as a mermaid; and cowrie shells are used to represent her vast wealth. Yemoja is also a protector of mothers and children, and women pray to her to cure infertility. The crescent moon and all matters of the feminine are under her domain.

 Call on Yemoja when you want to surrender your weary thoughts, and allow her to carry your worries away. Connect with her at the ocean and with offerings of white roses.

Reinvention

Bast

ORIGIN: *Egyptian*

MYTHOLOGY: Bast is an Egyptian cat goddess who rules over sex, magic, and pleasure. She first appeared as a lioness goddess and protector of Egyptians in battle. As domestic cats gained more status and prominence in Egyptian culture, revered for being noble and clean and for controlling the rodent population—and hence protecting the human population from disease—Bast evolved into a cat goddess. Cats are sacred to her and the Egyptians and were protected and even mummified in tombs.

A lover of pleasure and beauty, Bast is honored with a glorious temple built in Bubastis, an ancient capital of Egypt. She's celebrated during a wild festival every year, where boats sail up the Nile to her temple. The boats mostly carry women, as Bast oversees female sexuality, and they dance wildly and lift up their skirts to make festival celebrators gathered on shore laugh; laughter, which Bast loves, chases out grief and brings on healing.

 Call on Bast when you want to rediscover the joys of laughter and pleasure to move through your own grief.

Chalchiuhtlicue

ORIGIN: *Aztec*

MYTHOLOGY: Goddess of the water, Chalchiuhtlicue holds dominion over oceans, rivers, lakes, and other bodies of water. Her name translates to "she of the jade skirt," a reference to all the shimmering, turquoise waters she rules. Married to the rain god Tlaloc, together they ruled over the fourth world that existed before ours. Chalchiuhtlicue became furious with the wickedness of the humans in that world and released a flood that destroyed all life—except for those who were righteous; those she transformed into fish to survive the flood or allowed them to walk over a rainbow bridge to the new world. She blessed this new cycle of life we're in on Earth after the purification and gave her gift of fertility to all living beings.

Chalchiuhtlicue is often portrayed as a beautiful young woman, crowned in blue feathers and jade jewelry, with a skirt covered in lilies. Since she rules over waters, she's a favored goddess for farmers who need fresh water to grow crops as well as travelers who sail across the salty oceans. Chalchiuhtlicue also oversees childbirth, as the Aztecs often associated the womb with water.

 Call on Chalchiuhtlicue when you're seeking a fresh start, when you want to let go of the past to move forward into a brand-new future.

Estsanatlehi

ORIGIN: *Native American*

MYTHOLOGY: Goddess of the sky and earth, Estsanatlehi is the Navajo and Apache name for the Native American spirit also known as the Changing Woman or the Turquoise Woman. Married to the sun, she lives in a turquoise palace on the western horizon where she receives her husband at the end of each day. She changes from a young maiden in the spring and summer, to a mother figure in the fall, and then finally to an elderly woman in the winter, which is when she starts to walk west to meet and merge with her young self to begin the cycle again. Estsanatlehi represents the life cycle of the ever-changing Earth and all the living plants and creatures on it.

She created the different Native American clans from the dust off her body, and she gave birth to two warrior sons who used magical weapons from their father to defeat many of the monsters on Earth. To remind people to appreciate her blessings, she allowed four monsters to survive: age, winter, poverty, and famine.

 Call on Estsanatlehi when you need support in a transformational period of your life, and when you want to connect with your younger spirit. Use turquoise to honor and call upon her.

Hel

ORIGIN: *Norse*

MYTHOLOGY: Goddess of the Underworld, Hel was flung to the realm of death by Odin after a prophecy predicted she and her brother would bring down the Aesir. There she became its queen and manifested as half human and half corpse. She rides a black horse in the night, calling out the names of those who will be dead by morning. When their spirits leave their bodies, Hel gathers the dead in her warm arms and takes them to her bleak, misty realm, Helheim. Soldiers who died in battle and sailors lost at sea went to different regions of the afterlife, but everyone else went with Hel into her endless desolation.

Call on Hel when it's time to acknowledge an ending and start a new beginning; she symbolizes two opposites coming together to meet a whole.

Hina

ORIGIN: *Polynesian*

MYTHOLOGY: One of the earliest goddesses in Polynesian mythology, the moon goddess Hina has many stories surrounding her legend. As guardian of the moon, Hina oversees all the phases of life—from conception to death and rebirth. She also represents different phases of female life. Hina is sometimes portrayed as the first woman, a dawn maiden, or a guardian of the land of the dead—each manifestation changing with the moon phases.

Also goddess of the ocean and healing, Hina is the mother of all reef life and blessed mortals with the bounty of the sea—which offers restorative food and powerful medicine. Legend has it that Hina started life off on Earth, creating bark cloth and toiling away, but she grew tired of being underappreciated so she packed up her things and moved to the moon. Another story claims that she had been lovers with Tuna, the god of eels, and when she grew bored with him, she went to seek out another lover and became entangled with Maui, a great Hawai'ian hero. When Tuna and Maui fought over Hina, Tuna lost, and Maui buried his body in the sand, from which sprang the first coconut tree.

 Call on Hina for strength and courage before a big change.

Hsi Wang Mu

ORIGIN: *Chinese*

MYTHOLOGY: One of the most ancient goddesses, and most revered during the Tang Dynasty more than 2,000 years ago, Hsi Wang Mu is known as the Queen Mother of the West. In Chinese beliefs, the West represents all things mythical, magical, and mysterious. It also represents the setting sun, the waning moon, and the crossing over of souls to the afterlife. Hsi Wang Mu oversaw all these things and was the ultimate embodiment of yin in yin and yang. Yin is the ultimate female power, represented by darkness and the outer realm.

Hsi Wang Mu was also the goddess of life, death, rebirth, and eternal life. According to the legend, she lives in a golden palace on a jade mountain, attended by beautiful fairies and her spirit animals of white tigers, leopards, and nine-tailed foxes. Next to her palace is a Turquoise Pond, a Western Paradise where dead souls go after they leave this earthly plane. She is also the keeper of sacred peach trees that grow immortal fruit every 3,000 years. When the peaches are ripe, she throws herself a birthday party and invites all the gods and goddesses, who attend in order to feast on the peaches and keep their immortality.

Call on Hsi Wang Mu when you need to renew your vitality and when crossing over into a new endeavor.

Ixchel

ORIGIN: *Mayan*

MYTHOLOGY: Beautiful moon goddess of creativity, Ixchel also oversees water, fertility, and fate. Once upon a time, she fell in love with the Sun and they became lovers. Their affair caused great chaos on Earth; the waves became wild and flooded the land. Ixchel's angry grandfather struck her with a lightning bolt, killing her. She fell to Earth, where dragonflies mourned over her body for thirteen days before she came back to life.

Returning to the Sun, she discovered that he was a jealous lover, constantly accusing her of being in love with others, such as his brother the Morning Star. Ixchel left the Sun and created a new life as an independent goddess, protecting women and fertility—especially those on her sacred island of Cozumel. Often portrayed in the three aspects of the feminine divine—maiden, mother, and crone—Ixchel is the mother of reinvention and removing obstacles.

 Call on Ixchel when you want to clear your path and find another way.

Nyai Loro Kidul

ORIGIN: *Indonesian*

MYTHOLOGY: The mermaid goddess of Java, Nyai Loro Kidul was originally a mortal princess when her father married a wicked woman who became her stepmother. Jealous of her exceptional beauty, the stepmother poisoned Nyai Loro Kidul's bathwater one night, which caused her entire body to erupt in painful, disfiguring boils. Banished from the kingdom because of her now hideous appearance, the princess wandered the forests until she reached the south shore of the island. A voice called out to her from the green seas, telling her to jump into the water to heal her wounds and become a goddess. She dove in and emerged more beautiful than ever, transforming into her full divine mermaid form.

Now the people of Java pay her offerings of fresh flowers, shells, and fruit, tossing the gifts into the water. She lives in the South Seas, attended by a court of nymphs and fairies. Humans don't swim in those seas lest she catch them and take them back to her court. Nyai Loro Kidul is especially fond of young, handsome men in green swim trunks, her sacred favorite color (also the color of her hair).

 Call on Nyai Loro Kidul in a time of transformation, when you're ready to step into the next level of your life.

Sekhmet

ORIGIN: *Egyptian*

MYTHOLOGY: The lioness goddess of destruction and healing, Sekhmet is a fierce and ambitious spirit of ancient Egypt. One of the female counterparts of the sun god Ra (known as the Eye of Ra), she is often found protecting warriors on the battlefield. Legend has it that her hot breath created the desert. Once, she was so angry with humans that she brought on a plague that blew in with the desert wind; she couldn't be stopped until Ra subdued her with a jug of beer mixed with pomegranate juice. In her rage through the desert, Sekhmet stumbled upon the jug; she took a drink and fell asleep. When she woke up, her rage was gone.

Although known for her destructive and powerful side, Sekhmet is also one of the most powerful and proactive healers in the pantheon. She appears in dreams of those with illnesses to perform magical healing; she appears without being petitioned, though offerings must be paid later. Beer and pomegranate juice, arrows, silver medical tools, and incense are popular gifts for Sekhmet.

Call on Sekhmet when you need deep healing and strength; she reminds you that you are stronger than you think you are.

Xochiquetzal

ORIGIN: *Aztec*

MYTHOLOGY: A beautiful flower goddess of creativity, love, death, and sexuality, Xochiquetzal is a revered spirit of feminine energy. She loves flowers, her favorite being marigolds, whose feathery petals are a direct translation of her name (meaning "precious feather flower"). Marigolds also symbolize the birth, bloom, and wilting to seed to grow the next generation in the cycle of life.

Xochiquetzal is the patron goddess of artists and created all arts and crafts on Earth. The day on the Aztec calendar set aside to worship her is dedicated to creating something beautiful, and Xochiquetzal is celebrated during a festival at night where people wear animal masks and flowers. Always portrayed as a young beautiful woman, she wears a bright quetzal feather headdress, a nod to her namesake. Butterflies, which help pollinate plants and flowers, are also her sacred animals. According to her myths, Xochiquetzal's womb was bitten by a bat, which created the first menstruation. From that, the first flowers also bloomed from the earth. She guards the Tree of Life in Tamoanchán (Aztec paradise). Legend has it that one touch of the tree's flowers will grant you happiness, loyalty, and fortune.

 Call on Xochiquetzal when you want blessings as you set out to create something beautiful; surround yourself with marigolds to call her in.

References

Dror, Olga. *Cult, Culture, and Authority: Princess Liễu Hạnh in Vietnamese History.* Honolulu: University of Hawai'i Press, 2007.

Illes, Judika. *Encyclopedia of Spirits: The Ultimate Guide to the Magic of Fairies, Genies, Demons, Ghosts, Gods & Goddesses.* New York: HarperCollins, 2009.

Loar, Julie. *Goddesses for Every Day: Exploring the Wisdom and Power of the Divine Feminine around the World.* Novato, CA: New World Library, 2008.

Monaghan, Patricia. *The New Book of Goddesses & Heroines.* St. Paul, MN: Llewellyn Publications, 1997.

Monaghan, Patricia. *Encyclopedia of Goddesses & Heroines.* Novato, CA: New World Library, 2014.

Murrell, Nathaniel Samuel. *Afro-Caribbean Religions: An Introduction to Their Historical, Cultural, and Sacred Traditions.* Philadelphia: Temple University Press, 2010.

Mutén, Burleigh. *Goddesses: A World of Myth and Magic.* Cambridge, MA: Barefoot Books, 2003.

Sanders, Tao Tao Liu. *Dragons, Gods & Spirits from Chinese Mythology.* London: P. Lowe, 1980.

Skye, Michelle. *Goddess Afoot!: Practicing Magic with Celtic & Norse Goddesses.* Woodbury, MN: Llewellyn Publications, 2008.

Waldherr, Kris. *The Book of Goddesses: A Celebration of the Divine Feminine.* New York: Abrams, 2006.